BLUE-TAIL FLY

MADE IN MICHIGAN WRITERS SERIES

BLUE-TAIL FLY

VIEVEE FRANCIS

WAYNE STATE UNIVERSITY PRESS   DETROIT

Library of Congress Cataloging-in-Publication Data

Francis, Vievee.

Blue-tail fly / Vievee Francis.

p. cm. — (Made in Michigan writers series)

ISBN 0-8143-3323-0 (pbk. : alk. paper)

1. African American soldiers—Poetry. 2. Mexican War, 1846–1848—Poetry.
3. United States—History—Civil War, 1861–1865—Poetry. I. Title. II. Series.

PS3606.R3653B68 2006

811'.6—dc22

2005035890

ISBN-13: 978-0-8143-3323-5   ISBN-10: 0-8143-3323-0

Names of slaves and infantrymen are both fictional and/or historical
compilations.

This book is supported
by the Michigan Council for Arts and Cultural Affairs.

∞ The paper used in this publication meets the minimum
requirements of the American National Standard for Information
Sciences—Permanence of Paper for Printed Library Materials,
ANSI Z39.48-1984.

Design by Kachergis Book Design
Typeset by Maya Rhodes
Composed in 8.75/13 Walbaum LT

This book is dedicated to
George F. Francis III

And not till then saw he the Other Side
Or would accept the shade.

Sidney Lanier
The Dying Words of Stonewall Jackson

Contents

The Scale of Empire

Yet the most distinctive, and perhaps the most impressive,
characteristic of American scenery is its wildness.
Thomas Cole, founder, Hudson River School

The wood that engulfs
an empire of stone
cares only to maintain itself,

to green again the decadent
progressions—discovery,
desperation. Our delusion:

digging into the earth
that submits only temporarily.
Eventually, the vine creeps across

the well-swept patio, up the walls,
then through, under the iron rails.
The overwrought towers bend

to the runners thin as twine,
and eventually stand only in memory
as ruins even the rats won't enter.

Cut back the undergrowth,
seize *the molding dead below,*
snip the limbs just at the joint,

the discarded apple will have its revenge
in the rotting—feeding the hungry
world that cracks the sidewalk,

sating the birds that adapt
to the landscape of cities
as easily as a winged roach
that nests in the paneling.

So let us go on—
swatting the locusts that decimate
the ordered fields—insisting upon graphs,
the architecture of command and sequence.

The ants have already mastered
the soil. Small emperors of patience,
they walk a bridge of dinosaur bones.

AFTERMATH

The Binding Tie

At the end of the Civil War, a native Irishman illegally wed a newly
freed slave in Mississippi. They fled to the pine woods of East Texas.

Callie

    I was destined, bound to go crazy
    thick as the needle trees were that first year—
    white and yellow pines, ponderosa, fir—
    the wind swept through like a sick woman's wheeze,
    like my old missy's every winter coughs
    that would wind down slowly from hack and hoop
    to sputter. Snakes brown as days-old slop
    slid like haints under the boards of the house—
    muddy skins the sun couldn't wither.
    Whistles blowing all around—and hisses
    under your feet. This is what freedom is—
    a sinner's poor choice between what slithers
    over the dipping branch and what you know
    will always make its rattle heard below.

Andrew

Made a rattle for the boy you could hear
from the new front porch. Caught a good-sized snake
and didn't let it waste—ate the slim steak,
fashioned a toy. Soon I'll hang a swing where
the house meets the tree line—from that huge oak—
twenty yards from the door. I'll hang the seat high
                                        so my dark Icarus's feet can fly
above this mulish soil, frog-clogged creek, shack,
and his mother's grief. Does she miss the pecker-
woods of Mississippi? Well,   close enough
there's a dry-goods store where she buys rough
cloth, so at least the homespun dresses she wears,
dulled by days in the sun, with seams that prick
aren't from any cotton she had to pick.

Andrew

Summertime comes—she picks the blue cotton
dress—pulls it right over her naked skin.
She's a bluet on stems brown as pecans,
and just as sweet. In the late afternoon
I press my face into her high bosom—
smells of yampone, muskadine, and heather.
I could lay this red head there forever,
with her arms around me, in dreamless thrum
until shaken awake by memory,
the sudden intrusion of years in rope.
Her master left a cow's brand on her nape,
I put a ring on her finger—
golden inscription—a loving sign:
    Now you're free—you're mine.

Callie

I'm free—I'm his. We find ourselves rolled up
like good corn biscuits come daybreak.
He smells sweet and sour as buttermilk—
a scent my woolen plaits seem made to sop.
I don't wear the head-kerchiefs much these days.
Not that he truly minds, don't or do.
He says, *You are beautiful* Ca-Li-O-
Pe (I learned to spell that) *ever, always* . . .
and makes me believe him. Today he drew
me to the porch to point out a rainbow,
I never saw such a glorious show—
I could make out every color and *hue*—
a present only my man could conjure.
He could make yellow in a piss-pot pure.

Andrew

I scrubbed the yellowed chamber pot, then lent
a mute hand   from purple hulls   to parlor,
even stacked a cord—there was no cheering her.
So I spent part of the crop on a present:
two pied lovebirds—put in a cage I built
with my own hands—bought from a traveler.
I hid them in the chicken coop under
the second plank and an old feather quilt.
It was work to prod her smile. Her eyes grew
so wide I saw the whites freed
from their lids. The birds were jade as a mead,
dappled black as loam, and splashed Dublin blue.
Though *this* land keeps me from missing what I lack,
could I live this man's life there—I'd go back.

Callie

       I pleaded, begged: *Carry me back today,*
       to Ireland with you—seeing as how
       there were no for-true slaves there, anyhow.
       English masters, he huffed. I huffed, *Do say?*
       So, I'm planted here, to have these children
       coming quick and know-nothing green as grass-
       hoppers in April. I blame his hound's ass
       that half are reds, but that is *not* the sin
       —it's those that look like *me* I can't abide.
       I think about all the trouble curried
       in this territory where a knotted
       head may rock above its own rotting hide
       at any pale whim. Now, I know that freedom
       is a beginning only, half the sum.

Andrew

In the beginning, some of the red oaks
reminded her of madmen with whip hands,
but I saw dusk sifting leaves like sand
through the fingers—breaking Missip's yoke—
that muddy hold.   She thinks I keep her in
these woods for shame, or for adventure.
But she's wrong—I laid the long boards under
our bed, and my devotion is   as certain
as the dog's thump against them. I won't run
and I won't let her run away from me.
Here is where I have staked my claim. Truly
the bounty to be had will be hard-won.
But the clay of God's promise has been found—
to East of Texas, we both are bound.

The Finishing Thoughts of Festus Spencer as He Looks into the Camera

Ypsilanti, Michigan, d. 1909

Berdan's 1st U.S. Sharpshooters

Dense topsoil.
Sieved field.

Spruce forest.
Blue bough.

Apple-orchard mill.
Cider-peel mulch.

Autumn skim.
Ashen smoke.

The clear and warring water.
Ships sunk low in the lake.

Wild blueberries shook down.
Licking the sweet stains free

as a finch's whistle.
Tiny pleasures, those are the ones:

The clean line of a sheet tucked
just so. Plain-spoken women

broad boned and tender—
their scent rising like cut wood.

The bite of that first fall apple.
The first apple that falls.

Will you remember who I was?
Is my cap straight?

I

In our judgment, those who have all along been loudly
in favor of a vigorous prosecution of war . . . have no
sincere love of peace, and are not now rejoicing over
peace but *plunder.*

Frederick Douglass on the Mexican War

~

My heart is not in this business . . . but, as a military
man, I am bound to execute orders.

General Zachary Taylor

Frederick Douglass Speaks
before the Anti–Mexican War Abolitionists

Rise up with thunder
dissenting voice, and take your
place within the pantheon
of righteous forces.

We are accosted by the masses
of assumed patriots
who wave their flags and leaflets
overhead—but we will gather
the names, we will record
the atrocities, we will
face the prison cell
before we will support
an unjust war
thrust upon us
by executive insistence.

Ample Cause of War

Up to this time, as we knew, we had heard of no open act of aggression by the Mexican army, but that the danger was imminent that such acts would be committed. I said that in my opinion we had ample cause of war.

James Polk, *Polk, The Diary of a President, 1845–1849*

Sixteen good men were found in various states
of dismemberment. We had to go.
They had given us cause. Of course
no one wants war,
but who are we to stop the wave
that rolls from the Atlantic
to the Pacific shore.
Mexico *will* meet our demands.
Texas will be freed. I say now—
we must defend and expand
as God intends.

Gratitude is not to be expected from the hordes.
But why not? We can be a friend to them,
a civilizing force. Damn the Quakers!
Damn the Whigs! Slave lovers all!
If they are not with me then
they don't support the principles
my country stands for, the flag overhead.
Let the thatched huts be felled before us,
the tiled mansions, pagan temples.
Let us pave the road clean for a new man
in the territories.
Let us bring law to the lawless.
Let us take the book to the illiterate.
Let us elevate the hodgepodge of races.
There is no dispute to be heard
over the border. Their borders are ours.

General Taylor Convinces Himself That He Is for War

None understand the ruinous challenge,
not even the Whigs who in the main
support his resolution.

The President's boots
have not sunk into this
mud. He does not wipe
blood from a shirt
or console a girl who begs
you to spare her brother.

The volunteers are reluctant, surly,
pressed as I am into their positions.
Few will stand against him,
"for who can arrest the torrent
that will pour onward to the West."
To even doubt
would bring down
the charge of the patriots
quick as coyotes on jack-hares.

As for myself—
I have wrapped the flag
around my flanks.
It is the girdle
that supports my back, so
let the protestors question me.
Mark my mark—
I will continue on as if
the President were my own father
and I the son, his to command.

Doubt

My brother—a Tejanos, died at the Alamo.
I alone remember him—
the name they discarded
quick as a gangrenous limb.

He could have come south
with me—further west was no good.
Foolish to have stayed—aligning himself
with the Texicans: the remnants of Tennessee,
Carolina, Georgia. They did not admit him.

What of the Cherokee—on their westward march:
white petticoats worn for shrouds
and the ascot—a hangman's halter.
What did quills in the hand earn button-toed feet?

Letter to the Governor of Texas

Sir:

I regret to inform you—I lost my quartermaster in the most brutal of manners. I will spare you the particulars, but know he was found along the Rio Grande. More dead were to follow. We must not hesitate. Admittedly, I was not one for war in this arena, but I am in need of volunteers to enter Mexico now if I am to meet our president's demand that the disputed territories be secured.

The annexation will happen albeit more swiftly if my request is granted. The numbers are not so high a price to ensure the safety of those who desire the rights & privileges of our very citizenry. Let no one say I am not a patriot of the highest order.

Yours Sir, General Zachary Taylor.

Notes from Officer Hitchcock's Lost Leather Journal
Found 1855

Monday
Our insignia
—a sword through
a cactus wren.

Wednesday
General Zac. Taylor is
straight in measure
as a hock-leg table.
He moved us in rows
through the dead
prairie-flax then
on through the thicket.

Friday
Evening—coyotes
drawn by our sweat
howl and scratch but
don't dare our fires.

Thursday
We fell soon enough
upon the simple dwellings
and abandoned rows
of hull peas.
The dewberries
we shoved into our mouths.

Sunday
Like a bludgeoning rod
of Moses we parted them
as they crossed the big river.

Monday
My bayonet—
a machete that slices
the heart from a palm.

Liberation

Del Norte, 1846

1.

Catch my reflection
in the breadbox tin.
I see dried maws,
and the eyeballs
of a pig staring out
as if candied.
So, what would you know?
I have the children—
yams from my garden.
I eat them with butter.
I am their momma.
Blood soup.
I slaughter and wring my hands
in the raising, feed them
my sorrows, wrap them
in white, green, red cloth—
daughters for sons,
sons for rebellion,
daughters for their daughters,
sons for me,
daughters for planting,
sons for the pluck,
each one
for the feast of mothers.

2.

You say,
*Wife, when you were young
I could touch you.*
So, old man
who leaves me empty,
what would you know?
I have the legs to draw water.

3.

Stopped by the curve
of an iron spoon—

I squint in the sun,
a baked corn face more
wrinkled every revolution.
I squatted to birth,
it widened my hips. I carry
a grandchild on each one and
a well bucket in either hand—
so what does anyone know
unless the earth rolls
a boulder from their cave.

Husband, in the last battle
you lost your arms—
I do not expect your caress.

4.

This morning
I stroked my breasts with
a pigeon's feather while
my fingers played
in the tufts beneath my belly.
This *old woman*
shed onion tears.

Before you return
I will have thrown away
all shining objects
then smeared the knives
with lard, and the mirrors
you bought to shame
my falling nipples
and keep my mouth
from filling my belly—
I have cracked them all!
Ha!
Ha!
to the spirits they held.
Today, I bury them behind
the turnips.

By the end

there will be nothing
of us above the border
but tallow on the burial stones
and the desiccated marigolds.

How fat the sharp-beaked
vultures grow on our backs
armored by suffering.

Our daughters lay along the walks
or float in the streams smelling
sweet of rot, as babies sometimes do.

Our son's expressions wither into ours.

Some of us will go further south,
rather than bear the humiliations
of Protestants who yank
the head from the Virgin.

Others will stay with the gringos
who believe the distances between
brothers can be measured by shades.

Three Hundred and Seventy-Two Miles from Home
Chihuahua, 1846

1.

Twelve days later
the army moved
out with only half its feet.
He had two and hands
that could peel cactus
or pick the edible flower,
so he survived—
sweating under the brim
of his hat and the weight
of his shirt.

In a year of dried
skins, thistles, and spider
eggs, men would leave
their shadows for dead.

2.

Before the pea field melted
to smoldering pods, she
wore a skirt embroidered with
camellias the color of blanched
tomatoes or a young woman's
knuckles down a washboard.

What did he think of her between
flags? A man no different
than those beside him, bound
to their muscled beliefs and
the sweating haunches of mules.
She was only a blouse
strung on a line to dry
white as hound-bones,

a musk-melon
patch, too common

for remembrance when
so much is staked, when
so many men die
staring into each other's eyes.

Pokagon Accepts Colonel Taylor's Invitation

Fort Dearborn, 1833

My father's vision: the sky a fog blanket,
a forest of iron trees, the lakes foaming white
as fish bellies—the eternal winter of nightmares.
On my back ride the three: my wife's Pottawatomie,
my mother's Ottawa, my father's Chippewa—
so I cannot refuse to go,
to negotiate once more
for the bit of land he may allow us to *keep*—
He must know that none can own this land.
His offer—two thousand dollars—
is worth less than two thousand needles on the limb
of an old and bending pine.

Colonel Zachary Taylor Has Pokagon for Tea

His hands were large, grotesquely so—
unseemly against the bone-china cups.
I gave him the option—*Go to KANSAS—*
That's the future for you, open spaces.
He couldn't see the sense of it
but was civil enough to make his mark.
He could well have written his name—
but why quibble? He didn't
have the spirit. No Black Hawk. He would have settled
for even less than we offered. His hands shook
around the white cup imported from the Orient,
careless of its worth.

The Escarpment
Mexico, 1848

Sometime after the American soldier
finds himself alive, alone

He pulls the stinking coyote
behind him. Its neck furless
from the rub of the rope.

A dog for his son. Jumping
fleas   fleck
his wrist.   Taking no notice

he continues. *Every boy needs
        a pup.* The side of his neck
thick and prickled as cactus.

~

When the mule died
        he made a bed of its gut
and slept under a canopy of skin.

He woke to the smell of bacon,
his wife's toilet water, cow's milk
        on his son's breath.

~

The dog town looks emptied.
An ocean of heat.
No dog's head peeking from

the dank relief of a cool clotted hole.
Midday, he caught a jack-ass rabbit.
        It bounces noiselessly

against his leg. The tin cup is
dry as his mouth—
      he drains the mottled hare,

      cuts   a waterhole in its throat.
Beet stew.   A man with a knife
   can live   to eat another day.

Something ate part
of the coyote—gone mostly—
even the stench. Buzzards circle.

In Private Conversation: Buchanan to Like Minds

Cuba is as necessary to the North American republic as any
of its present members. . . . Its immediate acquisition by our
government is of paramount importance.
Ministers James Buchanan, John Y. Mason, and Pierre Soulé,
Ostend Manifesto, 1854

Then we'll take Cuba for ourselves.
Gentlemen—Hurrah!
No compromise.
Outside these borders
we are unbound—
To Cuba! Good Sirs,
where the slave will have sea
and sun to keep him fit. Why not
a force to free the island
of Spain? It is in Cuba's own interest
that we proceed. Should the Cubans
revolt, we cannot resist aiding
our deprived fellows. We must lift
from the fair island's shoulders
the yoke of Cortés.
Is Cuba no less than Texas?
Viva la Revolution! Cuba in another's hands
would endanger our republic.
By God, we are obliged
by every law, human and divine,
to wrest her from them, for us.

The Book Speaks of Pretenders

... and mingle my blood further with the blood of my
children, and with the blood of millions in this ...
John Brown

There are wolves who walk as men. I have seen
beneath their hair to the pink. I have seen
what lies beneath my own.

Who was the whaler? how far back
along the chain? see how I wait
for the groundswell, for the dark and telling
surge before the vision.

Madness sits on my head, *like dead kin,*
as Grim George says, *like haints—*
there to keep me walking upright—
drop a bag of copperheads on you if you don't,
yessir. I pat the dear soul's knotted head.

When my wife's boy doubted, sassed me,
I laid the strap to his face. Cut in two his
twined lips that welted, that stretched brow
so like my own. Was it madness to demand he
honor his pap? Now let him turn his face to God
and know that he was chastened in His name. Jesus
took no less. Jesus spent *three* days entombed.

I built a root cellar for remembrance of the Hard Above.
I said, Go down, down upon your knees in the secret closet,
pray that He will forgive you and that I will forget.
A son is a trial above all others. God knows.

They are woolen lambs, my children. Given to me
to protect, to keep, this black flock. Madame Howe speaks
of this command as churning water and flotsam, *then*
the whale of abolition dares the surface, transcends.
Her pale arms tremble then fly up into the air
when she says this, as if the beast were in her own
gloved hands. Says, what some call "madness" is up to me
to train, to let reason act as my net, my harpoon.

South of Houston

My father said prayers that meant soon there would be none
of us left who were not servants to them. Houston wanted us out.
The Texicans bred like prairie dogs—towns springing up
out of nowhere, like dust funnels out of Chihuahua sands, pushing us
further and further south. New laws sweeping us out by day like lizards.
They grew to hate us, as if *we* were the masters
and the leash theirs to bite.

I I

There were blue eyes from turfy Shannon,
There were black orbs from Palmy Niger—

Henry Howard Brownell, *The Bay Fight*

Civil Beginnings

Men, remember we are brothers.

Brothers, the initial cry was civil,

calling one to one further on.

Let them retreat intact.

If the enemy is no more than animal

then the soldier is no more than hunter.

The battle begins bloodless

enough—the enemy understands—

the white flag is respected.

So it goes with beginnings—

courage is the force withheld,

but by the end brothers are no more,

and the white flag is taken—

a counterpane for the cooling board.

Darling Wife,

I was there for emergencies and there were always emergencies. In this first month I have found a true thing—larger than myself or us, more than the fields I never did love—I am a good soldier. Not an officer. I don't want to be an officer. I am not the head to send feet over the rise. I want instead to rise as one of many. I will have a story to fill a man's journal for years—a story in your hands to tell the children and the grandchildren to come and those after them.

Yours Alone. Pvt. _____

Grey Jebediah

He's gone Grey
though still a young man
and takes to drink before his twentieth.
He can make it on a bird's bite of dry
meat and a stew of peanut roots—
      "devil's joy"
in fine company, with   decent enough
spirits, considering how the year will
see its way out without
several of the boys—lost
but dearly remembered.
Such is the price,
he thinks, *It won't be long
now, we'll sic 'em.* Hardtack
stuffed in his cheek,
he swallows hard
and gives the living a smile.
His comrades return it—
take another swill,
then on to morning drill.

The Bone Boiler

1.

Down the street—on Seventh—the bone boilers.
Steam clots and heats the air to misery.
Dark as wet wool—the limp rags we collect
always feel moist to the touch. A white scab
grows under my nails and it hurts to sort
cloth from the bins, the back rooms, the wagons,
wherever we can, my brother and I.
We sleep in a room with the little ones,
all four of them too young to be useful.
It's Ben and I that picks the rags, and fights
the dogs, and we keep scraps on the table.
The children of the bone boilers don't beg—
they get just enough and don't have any
truck with us who don't speak any German.

2.

My brother is a man. Though not as tall
as most men, he is fierce in the alleys.
He punched an older boy, a bone boiler
who looked at me too long and too lustful
when I stooped to handle crates. I was bent
for those eyes but didn't tell my brother.
Yesterday, I learned the bone boiler's name—
Schroeder—he's helped his father all his life.
He doesn't mind my Irish tongue. He gets
most of what I say by gesture—a nod,
a hand motion, a kiss. I hate this life.
Benjamin is my brother. Side-by-side
we two have kept our family alive,
but I need more than a brother's handling.

3.

Benjamin has been called in by the draft.
He went it seemed with half of the city.
We've had no news of him since his leaving—
I have to go and I want to get out
of this city, away from you, from us.

He did not shed a stone tear. Nor did I.
I wore my hair in two buns, not the one
he was used to seeing. I smelled of bones.
The three standing with me looked guiltily
at their big brother, then clung to his legs.
Schroeder was out working with his father,
so war was not with him, but war waited
down south, *a war for Irish broken hearts.*
Dying for the Union—Where are *our* subs?

4.

The smallest one died last night—coughed up black
jellied lumps just like our mother who died
after the last of us was born. *Gave up*
was how our dad put it. Then he died too.
I ran all the way to Germantown. God
how I cried out. Jill was my favorite,
but my prayers went unheard, so I am grown
enough to seek a poor woman's comfort—
Where is the shame in a willing man? None
dare judge me. I mean to leave these alleys
and take the children too. If Schroeder comes
we'll have a chance. West we'll find a city
not ruled by pointed tongues and teeth gnawing
us, bit by bit, 'til we are less than bones.

Shadows

Toward finale life is thick with moments prior
all condensed to the time it takes
a rifle's crack. There is
a furrow on the general's brow
for each man ordered into that
sound

echoed countless times off
innumerable other fired arms, but
sounding only within the valley's walls,
then carried several miles distance
on the wind with no volley in between.

Nothing.

Just a hush—

a hush so soft

some houses standing
think the battle has yet to begin

or is already over and set tables
with whatever is left of the sold
or hidden pewter, like silver,
and lay steaming dishes of whatever
has been shelved or buried,
eat their silent meal, and wait
in the shade for their beloved
to return.

Fragments of a Camp near Yorktown

Edwin Strong, Union, 3rd Regiment, Co A.

Face upon face, my own
A ripple in water only inches deep
Days without rations, then a flood
Downed by the side of a log
Both legs stumped
Months away and maybe never
A widow wailing on, on
Sugaring season at home—
The sweet run to rot
Rebel barracks left to forest, to limbs
Faces spoiling the water
Dirty, weary, damned them damned us
A Durham ox, a draft horse
Through the felled trees, shouts
Feet carried off by shells, by hate
Desperate as widows
Woods of arms
Artillery—a spilling horn of plenty
Red corn raining down

1864

A Pocket Full of Rye

Confederate anticipating Colored Union troops

The trees are so full in this light—
green petticoats the balls will mow flat.

If I hide tonight, beneath a mound
of dirt I will still die, trampled

by boot, or impaled on the dark beak
of a rifle. I long for my field,

my plow, my good wife,
the farm and its smell.

It took two years to clear a small plot.
I took down the black gums

with swings I then thought mighty,
muled the stumps, fought the weed,

spread the mulch, succulent
as flowers. I miss my daughters—

hear that? a rumble—rage from the portholes—
and I would have it over soon and

done. I won't survive these musings.
Into the pitch   the caws,

the crows rising quick, as if suddenly freed
from some great pie, a mad and mocking flock.

Snake Swamp

Louisiana, 1864

The creek meandered
(as creeks are prone to do)
slow and dense as ribbon
cane. In this late summer
we are pork in earthen pots.
Can we go back?
Regain our initial positions
then turn our righteousness
upon ourselves?
Seems a better way to be lost.

I am learning from this
dread creek inside its blue forest
where the fly and its eggs thrive
while we the dying remain
as stubborn as the already dead.

I wonder about the units further
west, fewer mosquitoes, but
fewer trees as well—nothing to shade
a man from that yellow orb above
that as a boy I thought a grand
charioteer. Now I know it to be
no more glorious than I.
Just a hot poker
doing the only thing
it knows how.

Walt Whitman Reads to the Limbless, Dying

In a second story—
the monuments are low
rows of sheets that reek
of iodine and marrow.
Screams swoop, trapped
like sparrows in the soldier's
tent, frantic over bunk and mud.
Compelling as the need to war, the needs of war—

Read to me.

The poems rise as ether
before the dim, lip to beard
he whispers through a moan
the lyric of divine union.
Beyond the cannon's shatter,
they call for comfort—
a song of beginnings—

Read to me.

The ghost of an arm comes to rest
at his knee. He takes up the book,
puts a licked thumb to the edge,
opens the leaves—

Is the hairless stump any less poetic than the blossoming grass?

      a poem rolls as a song across his lips,
familiar as the clop of a horse upon brick.
Piece by piece a life is reinvented, as the song
cobbles over closed eyes.

Write for me.

Linsey-Woolsey

Gettysburg, 1862

I was hanging clothes on the line:
a working man's hickory, the counterpane of a young wife,
a child's padding.   I knew how to beat the offense—
tea-stained linens only sun can cure—
without killing the fiber.   Not a tear.   Not a rip.
I lent each sheet the same care.   Fair enough life
I thought.   My job was my own   as I was my own.
Some women had been snatched by night.
I gave heed to the warnings. I hung the laundry early
in the day,   soaked (indoors) overnight.   Had to.
   —a feed sack over the head no doubt—
Beat   soaped   boiled   rubbed   rinsed (in bluing
if white)   wrung   rinsed   wrung   dipped (starched)   hung.
Each load dirtier than the next.   They knew
what I was, saw through hair and flush   profile
of a Roman coin, sold me easily
as white linen bought to set upon an ebon table.
A soiled handkerchief in my mouth   a hand at each arm,
I kicked like only a mule can,   they broke me the same.
I was not my own.   Heard the clothes flapping
empty sleeves   trails of dresses.

1864

Dear Mother,

*Should I have left war to father alone? Mustn't
Johnny go for a soldier? Should I have kept to farm?
How I long for the pale hands of my sisters like
meadow butterflies upon my shoulders whose wings I
took stern joy in pinching.*

*Mother, you will not see Father again, and I will not
see him soon. It may bring you relief to know I have
been brought to humbling ground. The righteous foot
I laid upon you and my sisters, the rancorous voice
full of whiskey pride, are both gone. You did warn me
against the rush toward the company of men, yet how
I tired of crinoline rustle. They are sending me home.*

Your Loving Son, _____

Gettysburg: Blue and Grey

In the moment before battle

That whale opened its gate

                    unhinging its mighty maw
                    to swallow and to purge—

O reluctant Jonah
                    —doesn't God direct the beast

By the time I reached the ridge

                    the view was glorious

It was a marching song

                    uplifting

Pointed flags aloft

                    in the quick-wind slaps of a grey sky

We moved in armored waves

                    reflected off every tooth, point, and shaft
                    even the sheen of our cloth
A nor'easter of blue

                    what brilliant metal—

The valley gleamed and I knew

                    the victory was ours
                    assuredly—

God's hand would sweep us

                    His great palm would spill us—

Up and over them

        like a grand cascade
        like Jericho's falling wall

Glory! Halleluiah!

        Look-a-way! Look away—

A Singular Dispersion over Franklin, Tennessee

One officer in Tennessee breakfasts
over maps, coffee, and wagers.
His plate kept piled
by a one-named slave,
quiet as a grass snake.
She has been convinced
the cannibals are on their way
south. She has seen signs of disaster:
bulls mating out of season, bloody
cream in the churn, a congregation
of buzzards in the tall stick-needles.
She prepares meals as best she can
given the conditions. Her kerchief
is unstarched but straight to honor
the Rebel endeavor. She manages
an extra glaze on the ham.
Surely you do not believe they will free you?
Why want freedom? Who bought you
that good frock?
Who keeps your children?
Without being asked,
she positions the bacon, spoons
the gravy, grits, and pone.
Replaces the soiled pewter.
Cuts new tomatoes.
Talcs her forehead in the kitchen.
Maintains a freshness difficult
in the clime. Her apron is blue.
Blue is the color of clean.
Her mother taught her this.
It is all she remembers of her.
A dry, blue head-wrapping.
The dining room is cool
away from the hot kitchen
with its walls of pitching brick.

No one goes in but her and she does
the work of six. Her duty. Her part.
Her master reminds her *in war*
we all must serve.
Just that morning, he patted her
thigh over the butcher's block
as he said her name. She has come
to pine for the sound of him
calling her
by that one name. He says
_____ with a lilt as if calling
a favored horse that wins all of its races.
It has come to be the voice
of her dead mother, of her
lost father. It is the unsold lover.
The sound that does not abandon.

An officer moves his hands over the maps.
She follows them expecting an order.
She goes back to griddle
more cakes. They flap up and over
the way Master's young'uns jump
up and down on the beds
as she watches their hair move
over the shoulders like creek water
over stones. He calls her again, insistent
and still famished, wanting coffee to wash
it all down while he and the other
officers plan and make decisions.

She reaches over his arm to pour.
When bricks with the force of an
army thrust him into her bosom.
Her kerchief embeds in the ceiling.
His scream locks in the moment.
The explosions, neither the first
nor the last, will leave the others to die,
but alone, without this shattering warmth.

Each man becoming a singular dispersion
of limb and whatever he was eating.

Lincoln Dreams of Sarah, the Servant

Father Abraham had many sons,
I am one of them and so are you.
Children's spiritual

I said, *If you don't kiss me now, I will most certainly die.*
This plea made through the darkness—she sleeping
at the foot of my bed, her short breaths—perfume
of sea grass and deer musk wafting balmy overhead.
Something tugged at me, lifted my head from the pillow
and I protesting, looked down at the undulant form.
I determined to speak no evil but called out anyway—
to her—no longer young—yet it did not matter—I felt
suddenly the strength was mine to free her from the rusting
chains of loss—she without one child left to keep,
where I am father to so many.

"If Not for You"

Riots: New York, Detroit, Boston

Blame spreads like spring plague—
up from the mudflats.
Throws open plantation shutters.
Seeps through tenement plaster
into pots of cabbage and chicken necks.
If not for you
If not for you
If not for you
If not for you
If not for you

we'd be civilized men.
Once this is stated, jobless men give chase
with bats and emptied bottles, chains and rope.
The story ends at the point of a ragtag's gun,
and only those left with their arms intact can
claim an Irishman's luck.

Above as below the story
up one side and down—
North being South.

1863, Detroit Riots, Again
Recollections, 1895

Like patriots of old we'll fight
Our heritage to save.
Harry Macarthy
("The Little Irishman"),
"The Bonnie Blue Flag"

1. *Johnny*

Friends, we grabbed the kegs,
bat-boards, and hammers—
    alien they were.
What kind of people are—
look—act like—

That is why we went,
they were not of us.
Low as animals they were,
and we meant it
to be a lasting lesson.

2. *Timmy*

Down   Lafayette Street
      Fort Street
      and Beaubian
before the unholy masses,
filled the holes
        we emptied them:
       stoned   windows
           their dogs
           women—
happy to chuck a few
for the old sod—
damned if we be *lower than niggers*
               again.

3. *Bill*

We stopped at the pub in the Cork and celebrated—
To the pride of Ireland, may we see her again—
for her alone do we take up arms.

4. *Abigail*

It wasn't as if those women
were such as me or me mam,
or their children like my own
darlin' three.

          The haughty heifers
wore their finery to unwashed rags.
Showin' off!   Their black business
in our faces.   Our men,
          soon to be unemployed,
with them breeding like hogs in a pen

as if   Detroit were theirs
and theirs alone.

5. *Todd*

Get the—
we raced down the street
but I tripped on the cobbles
and could not keep up the fight,
but I shouted for all to hear
and limped along watching
the smoke and fire bursts,
clubs and stones
I did not question—

then.

1864

Dear Son,

What brilliant pleasure to hear from you. Your mother is poor in field but rich in the animal joy of a mother's protective desire—to have you back in my arms to tend. Your sisters have both set out for the hospital ships. I and my own sister, your dear aunt, roll bandages and sew socks for such as yourself. What is a foot when it is the knees God requires? We will pray and we will last. I have my threads and you.

Ever, Mother

I I I

The pony run, he jump, he pitch.
He threw my master in a ditch.
He died and the jury wondered why.
The verdict was the blue-tail fly.

Slave song, "Blue-Tail Fly"
("Jimmy Crack Corn")

~

Behold the brown-faced men.

Walt Whitman,
Cavalry Crossing a Ford

Private Athens Descries

Company E, 4th, United States Colored Infantry

> *We are soldiers in the army . . .*
> *We've got to hold up freedom's banner*
> *We've got to hold it up until we die.*
> Spiritual

We are here to see this capital stands.
Freedom is a frog's tongue stretched long
and sticky. Red is our common color.
Freedom rolls over every lip
as if we *all* were slaves.
We are guarding a swamp.
There is a-buzzing everywhere. How
dare we gaze straight back at them?
Won't we seize the fair and weak?
Won't we take the dozing colonels?
Aren't we riddled with disease?
I cannot keep the mud from my shoes,
but my buttons shine and I don't flinch
under watchful eye. We must endure
the rain of ice and insults.
We hoist the flag each day and believe it
ours. We both blue and black
as kitchen iron, we
straighten our backs,
burn hot and wait.

Hannibal of Athens, Georgia

Contraband, 1st South Carolina Band of Volunteers

As Hannibal was feared—
I will be feared.

As Hannibal's name was lifted—
I will be lifted up.

As Hannibal was villain, then hero, then myth—
I will be as despised, as loved.

As Hannibal became himself—
I am Hannibal.

White Glove Test

Drummer boy, Colored Union Infantry

These white gloves are to my hands
what I imagine silk slippers are
to the whore's feet—cool—clean—
clean my good Jesus—I felt
I could forgive anything
in that first moment's pleasure—
sliding them over my rough hands.
Now,
what separates me from my master?—
with my back straight as these sticks,
and his ruddy knuckles less white
than my gloved ones.

Private Smith's Primer

Early 1864/1874, the 54th Massachusetts (Colored) Regiment

Aa—is for the apples that clean the teeth after a crunch; A is for the arms we carry—a shovel for the earthen works, a ladle for dipping up the gruel, a hammer for putting up winter quarters; for the arms we lost and may no longer use to wrap 'round the dying, or raise a hand to comfort our blue breasts; A is for the air we all draw, fair, nobody gets more than another; A is for the awful truth—10 dollars to their 13, though should a musket break our lines, our bodies will break as well; A is for the ash that fills the air with the stench of liver, throat, a string of guts like German sausages set a-sizzle, a-flame.

Bb—is for the bees that killed that drummer boy when he stepped into a bush full of them—buzzing—buzzing—bit into his legs that swelled huge as melons; B is for the blood that fills our mouths before battle, after battle; B is for the bush of *her* hair, the hair we dream and smell loosed from its tight plaits—black bolls pushing out bountiful—a halo we pull toward our bosoms; B is for the blood smell of a young wife left waiting among the cobs; for the blood that soaks the bandages after a leg is freed from its source, for the blood that collects under the ribs and clots in the knee when we run ahead, barreling forward—*Forward brothers!*

Cc—is for the cat I know Major _____ found under his bunk, fat with kittens, it crawled in seeking a warm place; C is for the coats we need, the cold cruel as a leather crop; C is for the candy of a woman's tongue—hard lick from a brown mouth; C is for the canteen, water cooling the battle thirst, and the burn in the groin where the cloth rubs constantly against a man's sack; C is for the cavern of shades— the valleys and trenches where Satan's teeth claim this human flesh, searching, *My Lord,* for a soul within.

Br'er Rabbit in Chickamauga

The grass has grown long.   A rabbit dreams he carries a musket.

None can hear a toed step.   He wears a cap that hides his ears.

O, boundless quietude.   He closes his eyes. Then opens to—

Cloudless eventide.   Eyes not of pink, but gleaming blue.

O, dewless dusk.   Without a seed of water.

The foothills mourn. Cry.   Blood tips the blade.

Bones green in the field.   Cunning—the hare that walks upright.

Yard after yard—the captive limb.   A rabbit's foot tucked in a boot.

Drummer Boy

The other boy being dead, they let me drum—
                    the sticks
                    were the stakes
                    I struck straight
                    into my master's
                    heart, I
                    drummed
                    to free him
                    from his
                    taut skin,
                    I drummed
                    myself free
                    of his cotton-
                    stuffed head,
                    I struck the
                    rhythm of feet
                    traipsing past
                    swamp, field,
                    forest, hill, and
                    foes stopped
                    as if dumb-
                    struck
                    when they
                    heard the beat,
                    the pounding
                    of my heart
                    escaping
                    the trap,
                    the tap-tap,
                    tatting—
                    t-t-t-t-t my long sticks firing—

Interview: Survivor, Fort Pillow

Well, I saw the chickens,
white feathers yellowed with dust
and shit. Not a clean place to step.
Grabbed one by the body, thick
of soft stink. In my other hand,
the eggs were warm. You know
that something alive waits in such
eggs, but you shake them anyway.
Feel guilty. Feel glad to have the power
right there in your palm to take
what you yourself could not have made.
Just for a moment you wonder
what a life is worth. I pleaded with him,
Don't shoot. Sir, don't shoot.
His fingers, white and red as ox gut,
shook. The bullet went into my head.
My skull took it on the left side. The air
smelled like sweat, but sweet. A coop
in July. I did not like to farm. No Sir,
but the farm was mine, free and paid
for. It made sense to fight for it,
for the having. A man has got to have.
Ate good on a morning. Better than army
fare and just as regular. So, I volunteered.
I was not pressed. Blood puddled between
my lips. I remember that. Like wild honey.
Like the bite into a bee flown into your mouth.
I spat. Dust rose up from the ground and the sun
caught every speck.   Every feather.

A Second Dream of Sarah

There is a natural disgust in the minds of nearly all white
people at the idea of an indiscriminate amalgamation of the
white and black races.

Abraham Lincoln, in a speech responding
to Democrat Senator Stephen Arnold Douglas, 1857

—at the head of my bed
her wool on the pillow

just beneath my chin.
She draws closer. The nap of hair

so foreign. I touch it
at the nape—repelled, repelled

it gives so easily   to the touch.
I touch it

again, so very soft. I see
its shape against her shift.

I turn over quickly, take her
above me. Turn again and press

down upon her. I know
only that I cannot cease

to stop would be death
to continue would be

the death of all I once held
dear   dear   *shhhhh dear.*

Nigger Pine

After the funeral of President Lincoln

Whether he loved us or no—
    we draped black ribbon

across our windows and doors.
    Our long faces, Lord, how we wailed.

Would he have had us remain,
    or sail off to some namesake colony?

No matter, forlorn, we mourned,
    even as we recalled the "nigger"

his tongue wagged to the press—
    into his wife's hot ear.

Perhaps our brows would never have met,
    perhaps our visage he disparaged

as much as his own misshapen jaw,
still, he resisted the lies of unwieldy romance

preferring practical solutions
    to peculiar situations.

No, he did not proclaim love for us. The old ones say
in some African tribes there is no word

for love—only action, deeds, and duty
    may say what the mouth will not.

"Nigger Pine" was the common term for the scrub trees
that grew on the blood-engorged battlefields.

Lincoln Speaks after the Bones Are Thrown

Mary Todd in her bedroom with spiritualist Mme Cadieux

Speak truly—did you love them that mourn?

> *All—every mop and cob pipe.*

And Douglass?

> *Even him—damned tongue.*

Was there one you handled with more than mere affection?

> *Never. Only in the freedom of sleep.*

Was I ever in your dreams?

> *You would not leave me to myself.*
> *Seemly devotion.*

Should I have turned my head then?

> *I was courageous only to necessity—*
> *nothing would have changed.*

They bless your name the name they cursed.

> *I gave them the same.*

Would they were all in Haiti, Father.

> *I am certain I would have brought them*
> *back—*
> *home, yes home   to me.*

The White Immensities

The Recollections of Jemison Jackson:
Slave, Runaway, Freedman, Lecturer,
Retired—Colored Infantry Union Army

1. Tatters
   1863

The clothes weren't the worst of it—
old nanny took up the white thread
and patched as best she could.
But there weren't much thread so
she would take some out
of the hem, and my pantaloons
wound up just under my knee—
not near the ankle at all. So it was,
that I was mostly in patches, covered
just enough for a field hand.
Zachariah made a gris-gris
of field-mice teeth. My wife kept it
wrapped in corn husks, tucked under
a palette of straw. I couldn't get to her
or it—'fore joining up. The sign came
too quick—a blue cap waving the all-clear
at the tree line—I ran until
all of my patches gave way and I stood
before men in nothing but my shame.

2. Cold Remembrance
   1864

That final winter it snowed in Tennessee
enough to stiff a man's feet to cowhide.
Sun didn't make a difference—
it didn't seem to be the same sun. No
heat. For days nothing melted.
We walked in a powder whisper,
and our hearts caught in the crack
of snow and fallen icicles.
An endless trample of boots
over frozen streams, the cold
so sharp it razored our coarse
cloth. To the ice-encrusted trees
I said, *Wife come walk with me,*
but my dear had been chained
to a white pine in Mississippi.
To the blanched sky I called out, *Lord*
I am but a man in your great, gelid
hands, come cure this chill—
but God's ear was taken up
by the masters of severance.

3. Take Me to the Water

The first thing we did with the reward
of an early evening free after chow
was to trot some upstream, strip down
to pantaloons and step into the river.
The one of us who had some reading
we called Preacher.
He put his right hand atop our heads   *In the name of the Father*
and one by one pushed us down   *In the name of the Son*
under the water and we rose up   *In the name of the Holy Ghost*
clean as a new day.

4. Manumission

—Sometime after having learned to read

The book left the feel of its spine
on my fingertips, its turned edges—
flushed my lips, brow, and cheek. Bereft
until I found the means to secret it away
with the others gathered in my small room
(every shelf weighted, every drawer spilling
its contents). In bed, I lie shamelessly
among them—countless women, men—
tasting the eggshell pages, courting the heavier
sheets with their stenciled illustrations—
a library I press to my breastbone and thighs.
I blanket them as if to halt a draft.
Is this excess? Culled from their bindings—
life upon life—delivered by the sweeping eye.

5. summer whiting
    1877

not smooth   nor downy—though fair enough
to frighten. my right hand shook upon that foreign cheek—
pale hillock my fingers moved over like the padding feet
of a bear, which was what she expected—to be mauled
in some manner—but I was gentle—fur where she imagined
claw and writhed so beneath me that I wanted to silence her
ecstasy   she bit my palm, her hips bucked
as if swimming   or drowning
she groaned   ye
                    es ye es   in so guttural a fashion
I lost my appetite for pleasure—
                    but curiosity held me up—
a lake of flax   the fish
compulsively swallowing   the water rising
                        just past my brow

6. Wife

We jumped the broom at sixteen. Of course
marriage wasn't allowed between us
that were slaves so we did it in secret,
in Zachariah's cabin. Being the oldest
at *God's Bounty* he knew the right
words to speak. Everyone laid hands
on us, kissed us, but no one clapped.
No one sang. She wore her one dress.
Her hair had been let loose
from its strings and sat in oiled waves
on her head. I planted a nose to her cheek
and she came to my cabin that night.
At dawn the bell rang, but she was already
headed toward the field.

∽

I meant to go back.
That was my intention.
They sold her after I ran. You understand—
the sign came so fast I couldn't have gone back
then. When I finally did there was nothing left
of our *Bounty* but ruin: the corpse of a house,
the blackened crops and Zachariah.
How did he remember me?
I ate an ear of withered corn, and lingered,
but desired only to be north.

Notes on the Poems

"Blue-Tail Fly," also known as "Jimmy Crack Corn," was a popular song among slaves. It is not known whether the song originated in the minstrel shows of the times or was an adaptation of a slave ditty recounting the curious demise of a master bucked by a horse bitten by the *seemingly* insignificant blue-tail fly.

"The Binding Tie" is loosely based upon a story my grandmother Vicey Smith (now deceased) told me some years ago about her grandparents.

"The Finishing Thoughts of Festus Spenser as He Looks into the Camera" actually combines the story of three brothers, Festus, Tennant, and Griffith. Todd Spenser of Ann Arbor, Michigan, a descendant of these brothers, recounted the tale to me. Corporal Festus Spenser survived several campaigns over three years.

The quote in "General Taylor Convinces Himself That He Is for War," which supports President Polk's prowar position, is taken from the Washington *Union* newspaper, 1845.

Poet Carol Was brought to my attention the story of Michigan's Pokagon, recalled in "Pokagon Accepts Colonel Taylor's Invitation" and "Colonel Zachary Taylor Has Pokagon for Tea." His story is "sentimentally" told in *Tonquish Tales* by Helen Frances Gilbert (Plymouth, Mich.: Pilgrim Heritage Press, 1984).

"Fragments of a Camp near Yorktown" is based on letters between Edwin Strong and his beloved sister. Their letters were given to me by a descendant of Edwin's, poet David Strong.

In "Dear Mother," the line "Mustn't Johnny go for a soldier" refers to a song made popular during the Revolutionary War, "Johnny Has Gone for a Soldier," perhaps a version of the seventeenth-century Irish tune "Shule Aroon," also known as "Buttermilk Hill."

"A Singular Dispersion over Franklin, Tennessee" is not based on the Battle of Franklin but on a tale told to me by poet Paula Roper of Knoxville while I was writing in the cemetery there.

The title "The White Immensities" is a phrase from Donna Tartt's *The Little Friend* (New York: Knopf, 2002).

Credits and Acknowledgments

Some of the poems that appear in *Blue-Tail Fly* have been published in the following journals:

Black Renaissance Noir
"The Binding Tie" and "Nigger Pine"

Infrastructure
"Interview, Survivor Fort Pillow," "The Escarpment," "1864, Fragments at a Camp near Yorktown," and "1864, A Pocket Full of Rye"

2003 Grolier Poetry Prize Annual
"Ample Cause of War" and "General Taylor Convinces Himself That He Is for War"

Mark(s)
"Walt Whitman Reads to the Limbless, Dying," "The Finishing Thoughts of Festus Spenser as He Looks into the Camera," "Br'er Rabbit in Chickamauga," and "The White Immensities"

2004 Wayne Literary Review
"A Singular Dispersion over Franklin, Tennessee"

~

Special thanks to the following persons who directly helped in the development of this book:

My husband, poet Matthew S. Olzmann, ever my rock without whom I could not have started or finished the book; my wonderful mother, Elaine Francis, whose generosity is boundless; first reader, poet Robert Fanning, whose knowledge inspires all who work with him; poet Paula Roper for her advice and help; the Advanced Writing Class (Springfed Arts), especially my instructor Mary Jo Firth Gillet for her guidance; my incredible family of poets at *Callaloo* and *Cave Canem;* poets David Blair, Regie Gibson, Tyehimba Jess, and Ella Singer for their encouragement; poets Thomas Sayers Ellis, Melba Joyce Boyd, and Bill Harris for their support; Andrew Ward for kind use of his photograph; series editor M. L. Liebler, who believed in this book and saw it through to publication; and Deborah Brodie for never doubting.